A Family Affair
my Bradford Childhood, 1900-1911

by Kathleen Binns

Bradford Libraries & Information Service
© *1988*

ISBN 0907734 11 1

Printed on low acidity paper

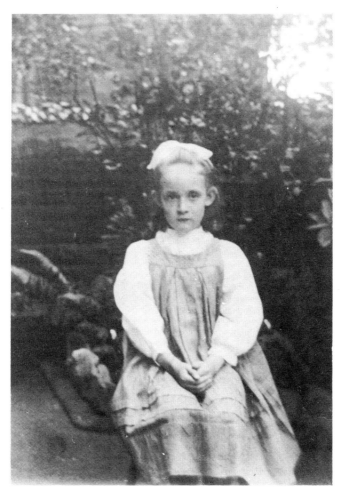

The author about eight years old.

HOME

It was in 1900 that I joined the family, making me a Victorian - just. My birth certificate, some fourteen inches across, embroiders this. It reads, "Eleventh June, 1900. 19 Athol Road, Kathleen, girl, Henry Binns, Mabel Seely Binns, formerly Spinks, Stuff merchant, Sixteenth July 1900" and is signed over a penny stamp.

And that was how I began. That house I don't remember but No. 52 is still home to me and very dear. In fact it hasn't altered one whit on the outside, for I went to look at it only the other day. The same bay window above a bath-sized garden, the same bright stained-glass door up two shallow steps.

Our family circle centred round Athol Road, overshadowed by the great fortress of Lister's Mill at the top of the hill. My parents had lived there since their marriage in 1895 and my sister Winifred was born three years ahead of me. Across the street were Grandpa and Grannie Spinks, Auntie Marie and Uncle George, and a stone's throw away Uncle Fred and his family and our other grandparents.

We were very close in more ways than one. Not so much 'close-knit' as the saying goes, more like a skein of wool, for we were bound up with the Bradford trade. Wool is warm and cosy and soft to the touch and a skein is loose but still all of a piece. Our family was like that.

Grandpa Binns and Father were stuff merchants in the family business of Geo. Binns & Co., in Leeds Road. They dealt with blankets, flannel and all-wool shirtings which was very apparent in our home with so many perks. The other grandfather was a grocer and he supplied our monthly order including a bladder of lard which we treated as a plaything. Auntie Marie was to marry a chemist in Oak Lane which was rather like having a doctor in the family. Uncle Fred was in the printing trade and by way of being an artist as well as a loveable clown. Uncle George now, was a little afterthought, only twelve years older than my sister; a very clever little afterthought who went to Bradford Grammar School and won a scholarship to Cambridge. We were a middle-class family and he was Someone to Boast About. All the menfolk were keen photographers, then a new and popular hobby, and they traipsed about with tripod and black cloth leaving us albums of sepia prints reflecting their life and times.

We all belonged to the Society of Friends (Quakers) and went to Sunday morning Meeting, attended local Monthly Meetings and wider Quarterly Meetings and were involved in the Adult School Movement and the Band of Hope Union. We mixed regularly with one another but very little with the outside world and were virtually 'brought up on reins' but we had a secure childhood and a very happy family life.

Being born in 1900 I can claim to have lived through six reigns. Number 52 was at one end of a long train of terrace houses all exactly alike. The back yard was used as a drying ground conveniently flagged for our hopscotch but we were not encouraged to play in the back street for fear of horse-drawn coal carts and milk floats. The front pavement was our playground where we could play on our own; if we went further afield we were always taken by someone, perhaps to the shops or Manningham Park. Now that was an ideal stamping ground with its lake and bandstand, its trees and gardens and endless paths and steps, quite apart from the 'Cartwright'. We were very lucky to be so near to what was virtually a slice of the countryside on our doorstep, not forgetting Manningham Tide once a year and the Great Exhibition of 1904. But that's a story by itself for there were real Somalis there in tents, not just painted nigger-minstrels.

We were so embraced by our large loving family we didn't feel the need to stray or go hunting for companions, especially with three younger cousins living close by. Like other Edwardian children we had little freedom but were brought up - I nearly said trained - by our parents in the home setting, to do what was right and proper, by precept and example. After all children should be seen but not heard! Mother and Father put a deal of thought and care into our upbringing, but I see now it made for shyness and a fear of the unknown.

My sister Winifred was a wonderful playfellow (and boss). Three years ahead of me she knew all the ropes and piloted me through the days and particularly the nights. We slept in two black iron bedsteads which about filled the bedroom and once we had said our 'Gentle Jesus' prayers ending "God Bless Mother and Father and all our dear family" when the gas was turned out we felt safe with our little night-light aflame in its saucer. I was afraid of the dark but against all rulings we talked in whispers and invented a grunting language understood only by ourselves. Winifred was a rare one for inventing stories and keeping me amused. She had a fearless nature and tried things out for me to copy. But despite her friendship I always longed for a twin.

2

The house was modest but four-storeyed being built on a hill. A narrow passage led from the front door into the living room with the drawing-room, its piano and bay-window on the right. Between the two rooms ran a staircase, steep and walled-in leading to the two bedrooms and the bathroom. The attics I can't remember but the downstairs kitchen is clear enough with its coal-place under the outside stairs where Father always seemed to be chopping chips. The black kitchen range took up the best part of one wall with its boiler and ovens. It also housed the mangle and peggy tub and a shallow stone sink called 'a slopstun' which I have reason to remember. For when I was about four we were having fun with a feather, blowing it across the kitchen from one to the other when I took a deep breath and sucked it in! It went straight into my windpipe and stopped me breathing. I spluttered and choked, luckily Mother was at hand and she took me to the sink, upturned me and thumped me long and hard till I coughed it up. Very frightening for us all. I've wondered since if that is the reason why I can never swallow pills.

Our indoor life was spent in the living room or the cellar-kitchen 'helping' Mother or playing with our dolls, never the front room, - that was more or less a show-piece. The back room housed our big square wooden dining table and bentwood chairs and a treadle sewing machine; the 'parlour' was kept for entertaining and musical evenings. *And* for practising the piano which I hated with intensity. We had a music teacher who came regularly and inspired my sister into enjoying playing! It was a dark highly polished piano with built-in candlesticks and was very ornamental. So too were endless pictures and photos and a bamboo table with four tip-up shelves used for afternoon teas. It was all typical of the times, a carpet square with lino surrounds, long lace curtains and green spring-blinds and an overmantle above the coal-fire. Not forgetting the aspidistra which stood on a white metal drum; as a treat we were allowed to sponge down the large leaves with milk to make them shine. This drum I found out later had once been a vast tin of Horlicks which my sister was raised on.

Athol Road was wide with flagged pavements walled in by two long rows of houses. But we were not an island. The lamp-lighter was a welcome regular with his ladder across his shoulder. He propped it on the cross-bar of the tall gas-lamp, mounted, lit the gas, threw away the match, nipped down and marched on. On rare occasions a horse-drawn tar-barrel came along, black and forbidding, when mothers would rush their children out to stand alongside and breathe in the fumes; this was supposedly good for coughs, particularly whooping-cough. In summer the watersprinkler was good fun fanning out water

3

from behind to damp down the dust. But the clanging bell of a fire-engine along a main road would arouse excitement and fear. Men and boys would tear after it on foot to watch those galloping horses and the brass helmets of the firemen.

Looking back, life came to us rather than our venturing out to seek it. But we did have unexpected surprises like the hurdy-gurdy man with his monkey, or a German band marching along the road, hat in hand. Maybe a funeral would pass with its all-black hearse and horses, black feathers waving on their heads, when, as a mark of respect, the street drew down its blinds. The relatives too went into deep mourning which they wore for weeks before going into purple, while the men-folk had black arm-bands. Once, so I'm told, a man brought along his dancing bear, a huge creature swaying on its back legs and fastened by a chain. He called out "A bed for a bear! A bed for a bear!" and the very thought, let alone the sight, terrified me for weeks.

At the end of the road in Oak Lane were our shops, one of everything, there was no need to go into Bradford. The barber at one corner with his striped red and white pole, the stationers at the other. Mrs. Fawcett sold clothing and haberdashery and the shoe-maker really did make shoes to order. We always used baskets, all shapes and sizes in rush and willow, and goods were of course bought loose and weighed in your presence on balance scales. Flour was in great demand as all bread, pastry, cakes and biscuits were home-made in coal-fire ovens. Wide wooden counters were a part of the shop dividing customer from salesman and very little was on show. A shop-keeper, anxious to please, gave you his personal attention and would disappear into his stockroom to come back with a range of goods to choose from. It was a time-consuming job all this weighing and packaging; butter came from a cask and was patted into shape with ribbed 'scotch hands'. All fruit and vegetables were seasonal, often local, and that first sour orange rolled soft and sucked through a sugar lump was a great treat around Christmas.

But it was the sweet shop that interested us most when we got our Saturday pennies. Sweets were kept in huge glass jars and were weighed out loose. The shopkeeper took a square of white paper, twisted it round his hand to make a cone, nipped up the tail and tipped the sweets in from his brass scale-pan, then screwed up the top. 'Spice' had a few variations but we all knew our favourites. There were aniseed balls, toffee-sticks in strips, hundreds and thousands, pear-shaped pear drops and acid acid-drops, humbugs, japs, cachous, chocolate drops and 'cigarettes', licorice bootlaces and licorice root too to suck that looked like a twig, but chocolates were a rarity. Toffee and nougat

4

came in blocks in a shallow tray to be broken up with a special brass hammer. But 'spanish juice' was my choice. You bought a lump looking like tar, put it in a small bottle with water and shook it about until it frothed, than drank it. Both our grandpas kept sweets in their pockets but we didn't think much of them though of course never refused an offer. Grandpa Binns specialised in Pomfret cakes and black currant jujubes, the other in tasteless thin glycerine and lemon gums.

Yes, life was very self-contained in Athol Road. We were not encouraged to play with strangers - but we didn't feel deprived, we knew no other way of life. We had our dolls, our toys and books, and above all our big family around us who cherished and looked after us every day of the year.

CHAPTER II
FATHER

Father was always called Father, never Dad or Daddy. This was typical of an age when fathers were head of the family, the bread-winners, and remote from the domestic side of home life; they had to be respected. Ours though was exceptional in the way he helped Mother with the fires, put us to bed and wasn't ashamed to be seen out with a shopping basket. He was very fond of us but we didn't go out of our way to displease him and what he said drove home. Not that we were ever spanked, only severely reprimanded. His admonishments were legion. Recently I jotted down what I could remember from childhood and soon filled a page.

"Keep a stiff upper lip".

"Come on. Don't half do a thing".

"Put you best foot foremost".

"Show what you're made of".

"Don't shilly-shally".

"Make a good fist at it".

"Put some weft into it".

"If you're going to do a thing do it properly, or don't do it at all".

All of which showed he was a perfectionist - and perfectionists can be difficult to live with.

What he did he did well, and this applied, of course, to his work as a stuff merchant. He approved of "hard-headed businessmen" and was one himself working whole-heartedly as a commercial traveller in the family business. Everything he did was done with gusto whether it was chopping chips or wrapping a parcel, so Mother would say repeatedly "Don't go at it so, Harry!" There was even puffing and heavy breathing as he rolled his umbrella. The way he stropped his cut-throat razor and sharpened a steel at table was quite frightening.

The warehouse was a background to our lives. Being a traveller meant constant train travel with his heavy leather sample case. As Mother refused to be left alone at night he returned all hours, often tired out. He dressed the part with his smart overcoat and billycock and laid great stress on a neat tie and polished boots. His springy walk and pointed moustache completed his idea of a successful business man. That same moustache was twisted to a prick with moustache-wax which hardened solid. We called the stuff stash-me-wax and didn't care for the feel of it.

Geo Binns & Co., had been in business two generations already and I'm pretty certain Father must have wanted a son to carry on the tradition - but he got me so that branch of the family has now petered out. Their main trade was blankets, white, pure wool and perfectly finished and they have proved their worth by being in use eighty years later. Their trademark RELIWEAR was a small silken tab stitched into one corner. Both lettering and the picture were woven, not printed, into the tiny square, together with the word RELIWEAR. In miniature were moorland sheep braving the weather on a high crag; a treasure in itself. Sample blankets with the same finish and edging were shown to customers to prove their quality. They were just the right size to fit a doll's pram so we naturally thought they were made specially for us! They also marketed flannel, both red and white, and all-wool shirtings in stripes from a coarse weave to taffeta.

Most things in the home were connected with the warehouse, like the blankets, Father's shirts and Mother's shirt-blouses, flannel nightgowns and petticoats as well as an abundance of stout brown paper and string, lengths of white tape and 'rolling-boards' (thin shelf-like wood on which the 'pieces' had been wound.) Odd lengths of shirting cropped up everywhere with a jimped edge to prevent fraying. Our stays were made from layers of assorted striped flannel quilted by Mother. Warm they may have been but they were ugly to a degree and how we envied other little girls their bought liberty bodices! Even spare cutlery and our best 'silver' teapot that only came out at Christmas were put away in pockets embroidered with feather-stitching.

Being in the wool trade Father always carried about with him the tools of the trade. A fountain-pen filled by a syringe from a bottle of ink, a pair of round-nosed scissors and a "piece-glass." The latter was a small folding magnifying glass through which you could count the picks (or threads) to the inch. One day a telegraph boy came to the door mid-morning. Those yellow envelopes were invariably dreaded as a sign of bad news. This one read "Lost scissors. Look coals. Harry." Mother at once got the message and hurried to the coal-place. It was one of Father's early morning jobs to fill the coal-buckets. He thought the scissors might have fallen out of his waistcoat pocket as he bent down. There they were, worth that wild extravagance.

*Winifred and Kathleen with the dolls used
by their father to illustrate his talks.*

The warehouse was an extension of home and we loved to go there. No. 79 Leeds Road was not far from Forster Square on the left and it stood back from the road with a front garden. It might once have been a double-fronted house for it certainly did not look like business premises and it housed all manner of exciting things. We were always weighed on the giant weighing machine with its square, ringed weights much too heavy to lift, and were allowed to print our names on the clumsy typewriter and sit up at Grandpa's desk and make chalk drawings. But our greatest treat was to watch the guillotine at work. One of the warehousemen would turn a handle and down came a long metal knife slicing through layers of shirting jimping the edges. It made us step back with fear. Father used to give us thick order-books with the heading sliced off for us to scribble in. There was also a telephone where we could talk to Uncle in his chemist's shop. Father often brought home different lengths of shirting which he washed in the kitchen sink. He was a rare one for experimenting and tried out different temperatures of water, even boiling and using too much soap to test out his fabrics. That tang of shrunk wool I can never forget.

But his life was not all work. He had another side to his nature and as a Friend was involved in the Society, the Adult School Movement and the Band of Hope Union. Being a rabid teetotaller he used to go to school halls and chapel schoolrooms in the evenings giving talks to children on the evils of drink...Well, perhaps not so much talks as entertainments. For, give him a platform, and he had a natural flair for holding children's attention. He was ahead of his time in getting his audience to join in, come on the platform and shout out. At school they normally sat still with their hands clasped on their heads when not writing. To them his moral talks were a party. To illustrate his points he had exciting things hidden away as if he were a conjuror. He would get Johnnie or Tommy to come up and help with experiments and was overwhelmed with volunteers when he brought out his many dolls. These were the usual wooden dutch dolls or wax-faced stuffed, all dressed by Mother or Auntie to represent a baby doll, a rich and a poor child, an old woman in a shawl, and a dirty, shabby drunk. They all wanted to hold the baby but no one cared for the old tramp. The dolls were packed away in his brown leather Gladstone bag and when the children saw him coming they rushed up to the 'Dolly-man' eager to carry his bag. He was a great draw in the poorer quarters.

But there was more than a hidden moral in these flights of fancy though I'm sure he never encouraged children to sign the pledge. The audience fully understood about the misery drink caused and the answer was in being teetotal. Father made up a song which our music-teacher put to music and it provided a romping end to the proceedings. It went like this:—

"I'll drink water when I'm thirsty,
  Milk or cocoa when I'm tired.
  Tea or coffee very seldom,
  Alcohol is best when fired."

And he literally did set fire to some alcohol to prove his point. He loved these evenings with the children and we too went along to join in and rather relished knowing his secrets beforehand. He liked to send them out singing and happy. His many 'lectures' were published with sketches in 'Onward' the Band of Hope magazine, for other people to copy - for they were most unusual and inspiring.

He had a big streak of the philanthropist in him and was interested in Dr. Barnardo's Homes. I remember going to one for cripples in Harrogate and seeing sad little children dragging themselves about on wheeled platforms and attempting to walk. This set us off making collections for Dr. Barnardo's Homes at our Christmas parties and their little magazine came to us regularly addressed to Misses W. & K. Binns which made us feel important.

Father also played the flute and led a small orchestra at home and at the Meeting House on weekdays. He learnt picture-framing and was also a member of a Shorthand Club which produced a round-robin of a letter all in shorthand; this meant he was an obvious Secretary on all occasions. But he didn't neglect his family and always had time to play with us, for he enjoyed it all as much as we did. Not only table games and drawing at which he excelled, but rough-and-tumble bouts when he got too boisterous for our liking. He was so full of energy he didn't realise his own strength and many are the children who remember his tickling all too well for his fingers were like gimlets and hurt. He was a boy at heart but just as quickly could switch to being a stern parent. Someone once told me "You know, your Father is hard on the outside and soft on the in. And your Mother's just the opposite." And they were right. Father could be deeply disturbed while Mother soldiered on.

He was a concerned Friend and took the business of bringing up his daughters seriously, reading books and discussing theories with other members. We were taught to do things the right way from the start, no experimenting. It was education all the way *and* 'keeping a stiff upper lip' but much of it paid off for I've never forgotten how to make a slip-knot or get off a moving tram safely in case of emergency. In fact a kind of finishing-school from the start! But now and then he let go the reins like the times we went to Manningham Tide. Then all restraint fled. He bought brandy-snap which we ate out of a bag outside among the crowd, and went rollicking on the roundabouts and slid on mats down the Helter-skelter Lighthouse. Then, all Quakerism forgotten, he made for the shooting gallery and showed he had an unerring eye with a rifle. We had him all to ourselves then, such frivolities didn't appeal to Mother. .

Father was a serious-minded man lacking in that fund of humour that bubbled out of our funny uncles, which we so revelled in. He might not be gentle and compassionate like Grandpa but he was secure and dominant with a hand for each of us to hold. I think one of Father's many inventions was what we called a Kissemy-smacker. All four of us closed up tight into a ring, arms round each other's shoulders, heads together, and kissed each other indiscriminately for a few seconds. A lovely family gesture creating a rush of affection.

CHAPTER III
MOTHER'S ROLE

Father might be King in our family as all Victorian fathers were, but Mother was decidedly Queen in her own kitchen. The whole domestic ordering of the house was hers. And no small responsibility either with little money, everything home-made from meals to clothes and the cleaning all done by hand, as well as two small girls to bring up.

She devoted her life to being a home-maker. She made sure she set an example for us to follow and encouraged us to help with every chore to learn how. Now this affected us both differently. I enjoyed it and have done ever since; my sister hated housework then and has done all her life. Mother was not quite the perfectionist that Father was but never far behind. She used to say "Don't just dry the silver. Polish it," and insisted when washing up that all plates should be spread out on the dresser to air before stacking. She made one slip she was never allowed to forget...The peggy tub was full when a leg of the peggy-stick caught on a garment and tore it and she let out a "Blow the thing!" such language in our house was unheard of, the equivalent of a sailor's oath.

Mother kept weekly account books from the start of her marriage which I still treasure and can refer to, disbelieving. Not one item is forgotten as she had to manage on a very small allowance. On the credit side is written:—

In hand	12/6
Allowance	12/6
Father for dinner	1/-

And on the opposite page. June 18th

Meat 2/11, Fish 11½	3/10½
2lbs butter 11d.	1/10
Potatoes 8 G berries 3	11
Milk 1/4½ Cream 5½	1/10
Ham 1/- Eggs 6½	1/6½
Yeast 1 Candles 1 Lentils 2	4
Firegrate 9 Wormwood 1	10
Bacon 9 Toilet case 1/6½	2/3½
	13/5½
In hand	12/6½

She sometimes added 'Unaccounted for' ½d.

Small wonder then our clothes were bought of serviceable material like drill or serge, and dark too so not to show the dirt. They were always made too large 'to grow to' with two deep hateful tucks round the hem to let down. But at least I did not have hand-me-downs as we were both dressed alike. Mother, when Mabel Spinks, had worked at Holme's shop in Darley Street at the needlework counter and was a master-hand at embroidery, dress-making and repair jobs. All our household goods and clothing were patched and darned till they fell apart, and sheets were turned sides to middle. She was no mean cook either as her own mother had taken cookery classes and Grandma Binns had been in service as a cook in the Dales. This put her on her mettle for the latter could be very critical and spoil any cake by pinching a 'little nip' to try it out.

Mother, like all other housewives, could turn her hand to everything and had to with no labour-saving devices. You got on your hands and knees with dustpan and brush on a kneeling-mat, blackleaded the kitchen range once a week, rubbed the steel fender with emery paper, polished the furniture with Stephenson's furniture cream in a tall bottle and washed and dried blankets and counterpanes, sheets and curtains at home. Father instructed her in the correct way to wash all woollens using only warm water with a little ammonia in the rinsing water. Hot water, of course, came from the fireback-boiler. White aprons with bibs and crossover straps at the back were the usual thing and little girls wore pinafores always as a matter of course.

Every day had its own allotted task or you couldn't get through the week. Actually, with us, Monday's wash-day began the night before when Mother grated the chunk of white Windsor soap into a special soap-pan and this was left in water on the hob till it turned into jelly. Then first thing the set-pot had to be lit with wood after ladling cold water in with the lading can. This for an extra supply of hot water or for boiling the whites. Oh, the things that lading can was used for, from preparing the vegetables to hair washing in the bath. Wash-days were gruelling affairs for everyone used a peggy-tub. The tub was wooden and like a barrel, heavy to lift when full of water. The peggy-stick was more of a five-legged stool with a yard-high post up the middle through which a bar ran at right angles near the top; all very smooth to the touch so as not to damage the clothes.

After the water in went the clothes, then the peggy-stick which you twisted violently crossing your arms perhaps ten times one way then ten times the other. It was extremely tiring but it got results. The tub was directly in front of the mangle and the clothes were hauled out and put between the rollers; by winding the handle the water was squeezed out and they slipped down into a wicker clothes basket at the back.

A mangle was really a very well designed affair as you could screw up the huge 24″ wide rollers to the tension required and the front and back boards slipped into two different slots according to whether you wanted the water to drain away or were pressing dry sheets which took the place of ironing. Ours was a rather special one with a chain drive and a handle that folded back to take up less room. We children had a toy mangle but the real thing was much better - so long as you didn't catch Mother's fingers!

It took the best part of a day to wash all the family clothes to be dried outside on the line or round the fire on a clothes-horse. Then came damping and folding and finally ironing and airing. Ironing was quite a ceremony I enjoyed watching. Two flat irons were popped up against the bars of a red-hot, (never smokey) fire then tested for heat. With a thick cloth ironholder Mother held the iron close to her face then flicked a wet finger over the surface to listen for the hiss. To produce a shine, a pad of beeswax was rubbed over the surface giving out banks of steam, then a polish with duster and you slammed it down on the metal ironstand. The ironing cloth was of stout felt laid on the kitchen table covered with an old sheet. Then you could begin - until the iron cooled and you started all over again. The starching of the linens beforehand always reminded me of cooking, for knobs of Colman's starch were put in a basin and stirred with a little cold water to make a white paste which mysteriously turned clear when you poured on boiling water. This was used neat for collars and perhaps serviettes but let down for soft pillow-cases.

All cooking was done on the hob or in the oven using a coal-fire. Getting the oven to the right temperature was another battle of wits. Pastry needing a hot oven was placed on the bottom oven-plate while a rice pudding went in at the top. The Christmas frumenty-wheat was left in all night while the fire slowly died out. If the wind was in the wrong direction the oven would not 'draw'. Mother then would daringly get out her cocoa-tin of gunpowder from a high shelf, tip a little into a screw of paper, - put it under the flue with a poker, light it with a taper, and hands over ears RUN! The bang was alarming but it did the trick.

All housework demanded energy, will-power and elbow-grease. A great deal was done on hands and knees like scrubbing wooden stairs, or washing and polishing the surrounds. Other things meant climbing a rickety step-ladder to reach the picture rail or leather a high window. Nothing was skimped. There were daily cleans and weekly cleans according to a housewife's standards when rooms were literally 'turned out' leaving virtually nothing in the room so you could 'bottom it'. A yearly Springclean was a major operation lasting weeks and causing havoc in the home, for every drawer had to be gone through and given new lining papers. I loved our Springcleans and was in my element nosing into little-known corners. Not much was thrown away for Mother had an eye to the future and her motto was "We're short of nothing we've got." A carpet-beater, of course, was a *must* made of coiled springy cane twisted into a pattern and ending in a long handle. This was used for rugs and carpets hung outside on the line, and very efficient it was too. All this laborious work was hard on the hands and Mother had recourse to a bottle of glycerine and rose-water from Uncle's shop, though Bradford water was wonderfully soft and good for woollens.

There were no quick ways of doing any job. Whisking an egg-white for instance meant separating the white on to a large plate, standing at the open door for coolness, then beating it with the back of a knife until it stiffened and you could turn the plate upside down. In the summer, when eggs were cheap, they were bought in quantity and 'put down in waterglass' in large earthenware jars to preserve them. When required each egg in turn had to be cracked into a separate basin to test if it was still fresh. Mrs. Beeton told you how to make every possible food for the family from jam and pickles to sauces and 'the art of using up'. It was all home cooking with Mother and only on extra special occasions we were taken to Miss Wear's cafe on North Parade for a desdemona or an othello, one with white icing on, the other chocolate.

The weekly bread was of course a time-consumer and huge brown crocks with lids were used to store a week's supply. To me it was all a very dramatic affair. I watched Mother thump and pummel the dough in its large yellow baking bowl, going at it like a boxer. I think I was a little afraid that those same fierce hands might one day land on me, though we were never slapped, just put in the corner as a punishment. And very humiliating it was too standing facing the wallpaper not knowing what was going on behind. Friday was a rather special day with a lovely smell of baking all over the house, particularly if you had wrestled with a scrap of dough yourself and could butter and eat it for tea.

Memories of Edwardian days are still very real. Clothes for one thing - navy sailor suits with big collars and H.M.S. Victory round the hat-band and coats with several capes like a cabby; even muffs. When our striped drill tunics finally wore out we were put into fashionable 'djibbahs'. These were all-in-one dresses with short loose sleeves worn over a blouse. Pretty they may have been but alpaca we well knew was scrubby on the skin and far too long-lasting. Party dresses had sashes with fringe on the ends but few parties came our way and we were left envying other little girls who wore dancing slippers with elastic criss-crossing over the ankles; no dancing classes for us. We all wore 'drawers' over our all-wool combinations, made of white cotton with bought frills of embroidery anglais. These buttoned on to our stays fastening the front up first. The back flap was made to let down when you went to the W.C. We had a little friend whose mother was so emancipated she was allowed pull-on knickers with elastic round the top! Our Mother didn't think it was quite nice.

Mother was devoted to her home and family and never seemed to go out or have a life of her own. True, she was a 'white-ribboner' (the women's equivalent of the Band of Hope Union) and wore her little metal badge. And she made garments for the Needlework Guild, again using warehouse shirting, and attended the social gatherings at the Meeting House, but she was always at our side and this was comforting. She and Father made a good team and I never once heard them quarrel though she could be quite tart on occasions and we learnt where to draw the line. A cousin told me recently that once on a day visit to our house she called my sister 'Winnie'. Mother pounced. "Her name is Winifred not Winnie and I'm taking you home straight away." And did. I think she took after her own mother with this sharp tongue. Alas, all I remember of Grannie Spinks is a little old lady sitting in a basket chair in cap and shawl knitting. She so often said to me 'If you do that again I shall give you a bit of thimble-pie!' Thimble-pie being a hard rap on the head with her silver thimble. Now Grandpa Spinks was a mystery to me. I remember him wearing a cloth cap and looking like King Edward. But how was it that in a teetotal family he kept bottles of stone-ginger-beer in the cellar and drank it at table?

Yes, we were very carefully brought up by Mother who was always at our side. But it was Father, not Mother who played with us. Mother was too preoccupied and busy and no doubt tired; her caring took the form of instructing us in housecraft rather than petting us. And it seemed perfectly right. I remember, one day when she was 85 and sitting, an invalid, up in the bedroom, we were listening to Wilfred Pickles and his 'Have a Go' programme. On an impulse I asked her "And when was the happiest time of your life, Mother?" The answer came pat, she didn't have time to think. "When I got you and your sister off to boarding-school." Dear Mother.

CHAPTER IV
AT '75'

When we were small with the family living so close to one another we could dodge about between them. But the best of all worlds was Grandpa Binns'. He and Grandma lived at 75 St. Mary's Terrace near the Children's Hospital. More than 75 years later I feel I belong there and my heart gives a leap when I pass. It was like living in a bubble, so enclosed and comforting, so many-coloured and beautiful, and where we were happy.

It was at 'seventy-five' as we called it that all went right and nothing wrong. Both grandparents spoilt us beyond measure. There we felt absolutely safe. I, being very timid, was easily upset and driven into my shell but here I could expand and be my own true self. It was such a relief not to be always on your best behaviour. We could walk there on our own, for it was only two streets away - well, you couldn't call St. Mary's Terrace a street. To us it was a very grand place, for those spacious houses were set back from the tramlines by a drive under trees with a gate each end. We knew it was a grand house by its wide hallway and shallow stairs with a shiny bannister rail you could slide down. And all the rooms were big to match the furniture; it was a real treasure-trove of interests and excitements. In fact the place was a kind of museum-cum-playground and what could you want more? And Grandma didn't mind you touching and exploring, so we were given the freedom of the house.

We didn't connect Grandpa Binns with the warehouse though, of course, we saw him there on our visits. He always wore a black tail coat with a pocket behind "just where he sat down". And out of doors in the garden of 79 Leeds Road he wore his Homberg hat when we had parties out on the grass or stood watching the Lord Mayor's Show with all its decorated lorries. But wherever he was he was the perfect companion and playmate, never stern, never correcting or disapproving but always gentle and sweet-natured. We did things at '75' we would never have dared to do at home, there wasn't a shred of fear when he was about. We even called him by his childhood's nickname, Daisy, a thing we would never have dreamed of with anyone else. If he ever did point out some small misdemeanour we would climb all over him in his rocking chair chanting "Grandpa's laughing behind his whiskers. Grandpa's laughing behind his whiskers'', - and he melted under our touch.

Sometimes Winifred and I used to stay overnight and that was as adventurous as any holiday. We slept in the back bedroom in a huge, high, double bed with a half-moon canopy over your head and thick red curtains to pull round and hide behind. There was even a stool that turned into steps so you could climb into bed and drop on the floppy feather bed which collapsed under you. Special watch pockets were built into the curtains on the bed-head and that was where we kept our licorice and violet gums to suck after the gas had been turned out. Making the bed the next day was great fun; you tossed the limp mattress about all ways to shake-up the feathers. When he was ill Grandpa had two nurses and he lay on a water-bed that flopped about in a different way.

It was all so fine after our little house. It had a big bath with wooden surrounds and a 'double U' that really was a 'throne' where you walked up two steps and were enclosed in a polished wood frame, and the plug was a stout handle in the seat that you lifted up, no pulling a chain. There was also a grandfather clock we loved dearly. It stood on the landing with a slow tock-tick and sneezed before it was going to chime. When Grandpa came to tuck us in, candle in hand, he always wound up the weights with a rattle on his way down. A comforting sound in the dark and rather like yet another grandfather. There was a loop-line for the trams on the road outside, which, lit up at night, cast queer moving shadows on the ceiling. And these were rather frightening things we were not used to.

We spent our time running all over the house investigating our grandparents' strange Victorian possessions.. the black marble clock on the mantlepiece with its pillars; the two dangling crystal ornaments which caught the light and made rainbows; the mahogany chiffonier where grandma kept her table cloths and silver leaving us a corner for our toys; and Grandpa's tall writing desk with its carved lid where he kept things like sealing-wax and a quill pen. The big round table there had a red plush cover reaching to the ground with bobbles round the edge and that was a splendid place to play if only the centre support hadn't been in the way. The dining chairs were satin smooth to touch but the seats were black horsehair that prickled your legs through your stockings and were hateful.

At '75' they had hearth-rugs, a tab one in the kitchen, very thick and heavy, and a dark red one in the front room. This was made in loops from unwanted warp threads from a mill and had tiny metal 'healds' fastened in like insects and which we were allowed to cut off.

18

There were two sets of curtains in each room, long patterned lace ones reaching the ground and heavy plush ones that slid quietly along a rod on wooden rings. The venetian blinds were of brown wood laths worked on strings; you had to be careful to hang on to the cord or they came clattering down with a frightening crash. Over the door was another curtain which worked by magic where the rings slid along on their own as you opened the doors.

The back room overlooking the yard was the parlour and used on Sundays. This was filled with exciting things like pampas grass, a what-not in the corner holding china ornaments, and a white skin rug lovely to stroke. There were pictures and photos everywhere, never an inch of bare space and a display of long fire-irons laid on the hearth end to end with a brass-railed fender. The chairs were upholstered and very grand and the square wooden foot-stools had tapestry tops. What with the sloping coal bucket and its brass lid, the display of dried flowers under a glass dome and the mirrored overmantle, it was packed with interest.

These rooms at '75' were sheer happiness and the meals so smart with the starched white double-damask table cloth with patterns all over and the 'casters' standing in the centre holding glass bottles and a sugar sprinkler, I always thought of this as a bandstand and it always amused me. The silver bars were laid out for the carving knife and fork and steel for Grandpa to use on the roast. Grandma's ginger puddings turned up regularly, steamed until soggy and turned out with her 'melted butter' sauce. She would have it the skin on her rice puddings was the best part being all cream, but I wouldn't eat it, it felt like leather. And it didn't end there for we played at doctors and nurses with Grandpa tucked up in a rug on the cane chaise-longue. We fed him terrible mixtures in an egg-cup rifling Grandma's kitchen cupboards for milk and cocoa, sweetened with sugar with the odd currant or a grating of nutmeg, and even a dab of mustard. And he drank the lot. What a dance we led them.

But our favourite game was dressing up. Grandma, for all she was not as lenient as Grandpa, allowed us to go up to their bedroom and hunt in her wardrobe. We took out her best black bodices made of stiff silk with the front fastening in hook and eyes stitched on alternately; we put on her skirts and mantles, bonnets and caps, her fur muffs and elastic-sided boots and paraded about in front of the mirrors and went downstairs to show ourselves off. And never a word of complaint. We fiddled with Grandpa's paper collars in his leather collar box, jumped on the bed and pulled the serge curtains round us, played hide-and-seek and poked into drawers and cupboards and behaved the very opposite of our home-selves. The freedom and the happiness at '75' was magical.

Now Grandma had a maid and we spent a lot of time with her in the kitchen calling her 'Annie Useful'. She was another spoiler and we loved her Yorkshire speech and her slap-happy ways. We didn't know of anyone else who had a servant to answer the bell. The bells dangled on springs high on the kitchen wall next to the row of polished meat-covers all in size order. Annie had her bedroom in one of the attics. The other one was empty save for the lace curtains hooked on a wooden frame on the floor to dry and stretch them. But she used to wash in the kitchen sink and one day I saw her stripped to the waist. I'd never seen an undressed grown-up before (Mother always dressed and undressed inside her nightgown). I was astonished and went up to her and poked her and she said pulling up her combinations "You funny little thing". As we never saw anyone save each other undressed it wasn't until I was ten and had a new boy cousin that I knew boys were different from girls. And I don't think we were particularly abnormal. It was Edwardian privacy.

There was no end to the entertainments at '75' - the dark damp cellars with stone slabs where meat was kept, the dresser-top which was 'scrubbed and better-scrubbed' and still had pin-holes of black which we picked out with a pin; the palette-knife that bent almost double, the big fish-kettle, the soda-water bottle that sprayed out a jet of bubbles, the barometer you tapped as you went through the hall, all so different from our own home. Besides Grandma had a drying ground across the back street that at the time seemed to us the size of a field, but which today is about the area of a garage. Here we hunted for caterpillars and revelled in grass underfoot. But how I longed for a swing between the clothes posts! We could also run safely along the front driveway under the trees romping noisily from end to end, so that once a neighbour was known to comment "Here come the Quaker warriors!"

But we had an even larger, better place to play in, Manningham Park, the whole of it only two minutes walk away. We went there of course with a grown-up but when Grandpa took us it was something special. He might have been slow-moving but what a dance we led him, up and down the many steps, hiding behind the greenhouses, jumping on and off the stone balls, playing follow-my-leader. He was game for anything. To us he was the sort of Nannie we read about in the story-books. He took charge and guarded us, played our games, taught us, laughed with us and the Park became a paradise.

And as well as all that there was the Cartwright. That was for wet days when we went in style under the domed entrance and up the broad stairs as if into a palace. Yet we went in and out as naturally as if we belonged there. Over the years it has hardly changed at all with its magnificent architecture and stonework to the black and white Italian marble tiled floors. The enormous staircases inside fascinated me with those tall windows looking on to tree tops, and the vast galleries with their slippery floors - they became home to us. The gold-framed pictures on the walls we knew by heart - Perseus being thrown into the sea with that agonised look on his face and the sailors toiling; Medea standing among the leopards and tigers with poppies round her feet - we knew them all in every detail, and they are still there! The Cartwright taught us beauty and sensitivity and enlarged our lives. We went there so often it felt to belong to us and Grandpa was custodian.

Weren't we lucky children to have such scope within a stone's throw of home? Come to think of it we were sandwiched in between the great grey fortress of Manningham Mills with its landmark of a four-square chimney, and the grace-and-favour splendour of the Cartwright. Both outstanding and a feature of Bradford's stone and built of millstone grit. I wonder if some of that grit rubbed off on us as children, remembering Father's constant reminder "Keep a stiff upper lip".

CHAPTER V
SUNDAYS

Sundays were not our favourite day. There was an unfailing routine to accept, as tight-laced as Mother's whalebone corsets... Meeting.

Without fail, rain or shine, as a family we went to the Quaker Meeting in Fountain Street. And it was a long, long walk in our Sunday clothes complete with white cotton gloves and buttoned boots. Every child takes its own home background for granted, and this was just part of life. We knew no other way; I doubt if we had ever been into a church or chapel and had no experience of organ music or singing, or the beauty of stained glass windows or even ornament in a place of worship. We just tagged along from habit and nothing was ever explained about why a Friends' service was conducted as it was. It was something to be endured, that's all.

We got there on the dot of 10.30, went up the imposing stairs and through the pillars and straight into the Women's cloakroom to leave raincoats and umbrellas, and say How-do while Friends were gathering. Cloakrooms for both men and women were spacious and well-appointed with lavatories and wash-basins, table and chairs with a carafe of water and glasses, and a horsehair sofa in case anyone was taken ill. The entrance hall was large and stone-flagged and a double door beyond opened into the Meeting House itself, a huge quiet hall with a gallery and a raised 'Minister's gallery'. Rows of benches were arranged in four directions otherwise it appeared quite empty. We walked in in a row and took our regular places, men on one side, women on the other. We sat on long plain benches and buffets were provided for children and the elderly. The menfolk walked in with their hats on and pushed them under the seat. There was nothing to look at but the 'worthies' perched up in front with their reading desk and high lamps. The doors were closed and the door-keeper sat at his appointed place to usher in late-comers. The silence and simplicity gave it a special atmosphere. You could feel the silence.

There was no formal opening to the service, we just sat quietly together. All we could do as children was watch and note, no one moved, some heads were bowed hands clasped, some looked into space oblivous of everyone. A foot might shuffle or someone suppressed a cough or opened a handbag for a handkerchief but there was utter stillness until someone felt moved to stand up and speak, passing on their message. We didn't listen. This set off a gentle stir, perhaps an exchange of glances. The children wriggled a little, they couldn't understand what was said but it relieved the tedium. Someone praying knelt down while the meeting stood up heads bent. There was nothing of any interest whatsoever for us, we took no part in the service but like the obedient little Edwardians we were we had to accept and endure. No fidgeting, no looking around, just sitting still hands in lap. But we could watch the clock and wait for the moment when with no prearranged signal one Friend in the Minister's Gallery would shake hands with his neighbours to break up the meeting. Then we came back to life. What had been a painted picture turned out to be real after all with smiling faces, voices and a crowd rising from their seats. And our weekly ordeal was over.

We were used to the procedure unaware of other forms of worship. It was only later, much later that we found that Quakers were different. No ritual, no paid minister, no choir, no music or hymns, no ordered service or prayer-book, just a gathering of like-minded people with a concern for peace and society who felt they were all of equal standing and could take their share in the ministry of the meeting if the spirit so moved them. Sundays was an extension of their daily lives believing as they do that "there is that of God in everyman", and that outward trappings were unnecessary. To us then it was a solemn and wearing obligation. How very different from today's Quaker Meetings where rigidity has given way to freedom and the children go out at half time to take part in their own activities. We sat solemnly through the whole hour.

But the bit after the meeting was another thing. We children were turned loose to run about the place. There was the gallery with two sets of stone steps to run up and down and more down to the cellars. Also the big schoolroom with smaller rooms off with folding doors, a large platform and desk all designed for games. To add to our pleasure we met other children including boys and that was a thrill for our all-girl family.

During the week there were Monthly and Quarterly Meetings held sometimes on our premises when we played host for business and social purposes. Meals on such occasions meant a great deal of hard work for the womenfolk as visiting Friends had to be fed. All the ladies were called in and worked in the kitchen in their white aprons and wide decorative straw hats. Trestle tables were put up and covered with white cloths. There were roasts, Yorkshire Pudding, and Mabel Binns' special apple pies, and even Henry Binns was called on to help with the sandwiches as he could be relied on to cut a long loaf into thin equal slices to the last crust - literally a perfectionist to the end. The business side of meetings didn't interest us but we liked to watch the clerk write and read his impromptu minutes in the big ledger. This was done without any voting or show of hands but by taking 'the feel of the meeting'. This really was fun to us as voices high and low, loud and soft spoke up "I hope it will be done", "I hope it will be done", came from all over the hall. All business meetings began with a short silence, in the same way we had our private 'silence' at meals.

Our duty done the rest of Sundays were a little shadowy being set apart from weekdays. No shoes were cleaned that day, and the barest of cooking done. No sewing or knitting was allowed and our only book was a child's annual called "Sunday". But we felt things had been worthwhile if, on our long walk, we were overtaken by Frederick Priestman, a wealthy mill-owner and Elder of the Meeting he went to Meeting in his carriage. If so he would pick us up and we clambered in and arrived in state - an ecstatic state. Sometimes one of us was allowed to sit up on the box with the driver watching him hold the reins and flick the horse with his whip. His horse, with others, was stabled in the side premises until the return journey home. We came back by tram which didn't run till mid-day.

But there was always something to look forward to on a Sunday - tea, just the two of us with Grandpa and Grandma Binns. All the best gilt-edged china, the silver toast rack, the outsize silver teaspoons and always rice or seed cake. Often there were pears for tea which Grandpa peeled delicately with his thin silver fruit-knife. We helped make the toast in the kitchen on long pronged toasting forks in front of the bars of the red-hot fire. You had to keep the toast moving or it got toasted in stripes. I never could decide when the toast was ready as smoke looked exactly like steam to me.

But the best part of all was when we sat round the fire in the evenings. Grandpa was the perfect playmate. Where Father would organise and take charge carrying everything off with gusto, the game wasn't ours any more. But Grandpa was a pawn in our hands ready to play with gentleness and patience. He also had his own specialities that we never tired of. His gold time piece carried on a chain in his waistcoat pocket would suddenly spring open when you blew on it. He had a sovereign case on another chain and we were allowed to handle a gold sovereign and post it into the spring socket

24

where it disappeared. But his never-failing trick was to ferret into a tailcoat pocket and take out his large linen hankie. He would fold it up this way and that, tie a knot, and mysteriously under our very eyes there was a mouse sitting on the back of his hand with little ears. And suddenly it shot into space and landed on the floor. That mystery was never solved.

Sundays ended with Grandpa and Grandma sitting on opposite sides of the blazing fire with the two of us on hassocks at their feet. The big steel fireirons lay crisscross over the hearth, the flames licked and flickered, the cinders dropped into the tin, the clock chimed sweetly and holding all these sounds together came Grandpa's quiet voice reading to us from Beatrix Potter's little book... "But don't go into Mr. McGregor's garden. Your father had an accident there he was put in a pie by Mrs. McGregor". Always at the same speed, with the same intonation and pauses while he turned the pages. This was security and loving at its peak, a picture which has never left me. His veined hands and bent fingers were within reach, the swing of the rocking-chair, warmth, friendship and that unforgettable loving voice lulled you into utter contentment.

And that's how Sundays ended.

CHAPTER VI
HOLIDAYS

I can re-live those days as if they happened yesterday. I'm five or six and we're going away in a railway train.

"Packing up and going away, not tomorrow but today" is what Grandpa used to chant. Holidays! A dream come true. An exciting break in a so-familiar world. A week or even more at the seaside. Our tummies began to squirm at the very thought of it.

The preparations were all part of the adventure - the getting out of the domed trunk from the attic, a giant basket skip covered in black canvas with a tray inside to take Mother's assorted hats. It held all our seaside possessions for the four of us. Then the sorting out of the wooden spades in three sizes all put away from last year which were rolled up with umbrellas in a travelling rug and strapped up. Our rubber sand-shoes we should buy when we got there, comfortable and soft after our usual boots. We were in a fever of excitement.

When Saturday came and the cab to the door, we had been ready and waiting - a horse-cab, of course, with the driver perched on his 'box', whip dangling, and the trunk roped on at the back. The clip-clop of the horse's hooves on the way to the Midland station was repeated with faster heart-beats at the far end when we drove in a smart open carriage to our sea-front lodgings.

Morecambe! Oh, the smell of the sea, the pier, the long promenade with its horse-drawn open 'toast-rack', the rows of high lamps, the little wooden jetties, the assortment of boarding-houses with their names picked out in paint - it was indeed a different world. And we extracted every golden moment from it.

The unpacking over Mother took us shopping for we bought our own food and the landlady cooked and served it. Filling the giant sideboard in our own sitting-room was like playing houses. And always fish for tea the first day which tasted so much better than Mother's cooking. Father immediately bought himself a walking stick from the tobacconist's, we fitted on our silent rubber pumps and went out exploring. Even the greengrocers was different with sawdust on the shop floor and all manner of goods spread out across the pavement. We saved up the final treat of going on the shore till the last. Then, oh then, the thrill of shuffling through soft sand, the scattered pebbles and the piles of empty mussel shells. We kept on stopping to discover new and further joys. Our hearts were pounding, it just wasn't real. But the donkeys were. The smell of donkeys as they stood in a huddle summed it all up.

Always hats to be worn, of course, big straw ones with elastic under the chin, sometimes sailor hats or red and white knitted caps. Father had discarded his billycock for a straw benjie while Mother chose one of her smartest piled up with feathers and flowers. Then that moment of glory when you took off stockings and shoes and fearfully set foot in the shallow water, paddling in deeper as your courage grew, with dress held high and salt water splashing up. Some mothers allowed their children to stuff their white knickers with bunched up clothes but we weren't allowed such naughty ways. Very gingerly we walked to and fro catching our breath as a tiny wave rose up our legs. We wandered along the shallow edges disbelieving this was all true. Such freedom.

Meanwhile Father with his usual business-like habit, got to work on the sand. He planted his feet firmly, took his outsize spade and in one movement swung it round marking out a perfect circle and began to dig. This was his holiday too and he enjoyed making sand-castles even more than his daughters. Mother sat by the wooden groins on her small folding camp-stool and looked on, fully dressed in shirt blouse, ground-length skirt and polished shoes.

Even the bedrooms were adventurous places. For once we two had to share a double bed. Mother at once took our the long bolster from under the pillows and laid it next to the sheets down the middle of the bed to separate us and avoid scuffles to come. The wash-stand stood at one side of the room complete with toilet set of large water jug and basin, matching tooth-brush jar and soap-dish. And sometimes there was a china antler affair for ladies to thread their rings on. Hot water was brought up to you from the kitchen in a small painted can with spout and lid and when you'd washed you tipped the water into the white slopbucket beneath. If this filled up you had to use the chamber-pot under the bed; and if in the night you forgot this you sat down in a pool of cold water - an experience you never forgot.

So many excitements to revel in whether at Morecambe, Bridlington and once at Southport where we rowed in boats on the giant lake. But Morecambe had its Strawberry Gardens where there were long swings and they were our prized favourites. Or there were drives along the sea-front in horse-drawn toast-racks to Bare or further on to Hest Bank where you could stand on the railway bridge smothered in steam and smoke and watch the passing engine pick up water from the long trough between the rails, at top speed.

No two days were alike, always something new to explore, different shells to collect in your metal buckets, wet rippled sand instead of the soft dry kind, the weighing machine at the pier-end where you sat in a golden seat balanced with weights across the bar or looked enviously at the building that Grandpa always called 'the sigh-to-matter-graph' (cinematograph). We walked along the pier with its echoing footsteps, printing our names on metal strips by putting money in a slot machine and then pressing the right buttons. We ventured down the narrow planks of the jetties leading into the sea and saw it splash round and under you and through the chinks and felt very brave as there wasn't room for anyone to walk alongside and hold your hand. Every day, every minute was joy and adventure, but the black "nigger-minstrels" with their banjos and the pushing crowds gave you a funny feeling. Even going home was a small happiness when you unpacked your sandshoes and out tipped a trickle of sand on the bedroom carpet.

The grandparents treated us to holidays and sometimes three generations went to Ilkley. The train journey was all part of the adventure. Now Father being a commercial traveller knew his way about the railways and took it all for granted. He piloted us around the Midland Station which to us was as good as Manningham Tide with its refreshment room and bookstall, large ticket office and men in uniform pulling trolleys. We felt like the ladies in story books who had servants to wait on them as the porters took our trunk and put it in the guard's van and waited for a tip. We made for a window seat and drank in every detail as we sat in our hats and gloves on the upholstered 3rd class compartment. It was a stopping train giving us time to read all the large advertisements nailed to the walls - BOVRIL, BEECHAM'S PILLS, OXO, PEARS SOAP, TUROG, COLMAN'S MUSTARD. The telephone wires mystified us the way they went up and down in waves; and if it was Easter we counted all the black lambs in the fields.

Father, true to type, took out his ever-ready scissors and cut all our return tickets neatly down the middle. Most people simply bent them about and left ragged edges. First-class compartments had blinds and antimacassars but all carriages provided mirrors. If you were going on a long journey you hunted for a 'closet carriage' with a 'double U' leading out of it as there were no corridor trains. As soon as the train dived into a tunnel you had to rush to shut the windows to keep out the thick black smoke and you shot into the dark, and waited for the tiny opening at the end to grow and grow. Everything about a railway journey was exciting - but there was one thing we never relished. A thick black leather strap hung down from the door window to open it and Father loved to tease us with it in play, whacking our outstretched hands if we weren't quick enough. Like his tickling it was more pain than pleasure.

Now the Ilkley holiday was quite different from the seaside. It was hilly and the cab had a job to drag us and the trunk half way up Wells Road. It was a double-fronted house and very grand, and it was there that I did my first sleep-walking act. I fell down a flight of stairs in my nightgown and never remembered a thing, and for months afterwards at home, was fastened into the bedroom with a horrid clasp on the outside, well out of reach. That was when Big Sister had gone away to boarding school and I slept alone. Nearby at Ilkley was the bandstand with its row of seats and noisy brass band, so on our first shopping expedition we went to a needlework shop and bought a mat with a transfer on and thick silks so we could sit there and watch. We weren't allowed to run about and disturb the audience, but once on the moors we could roam free, battle through the bracken, slide backwards down the dry slippery turf and pick bilberries. Grandpa always found an old envelope in his pocket but hunt as we would we never once filled it, they were so small.

Sometimes Grandma took a bath-chair pulled up by a pony up the steep path towards the White Wells while the driver walked alongside. Oh how I longed to sit on her knee and be covered with a rug, but it never happened. We peered into the depth of the Roman Bath and were afraid of falling into the mossy well but wished our wishes, and we were always at the tarn sailing our small boats and clambering over the rocks. We chased round and round and found hidden sheep tracks and picked the heather, but our chief delight was the Salvation Army lady who conducted an action song for a crowd of children to join in. It went...

"Our sins were as high as a mountain,
They all disappeared in a fountain.
I wrote my name down
For a palace and crown
And praise the dear Lord I am free-ee-ee."

There was also the toil and thrill of climbing up to the Cow and Calf and standing on top looking back at the midget houses below. All the letters carved into the stone had to be explored, some of them in dangerous places. And instead of Father's "Now show what you're made of", it was a case of "Don't be so venturesome". Those days of freedom and childhood delights were memorable, running unattended into the unknown, into bogs and hollows, streams and hillocks. But we walked, oh yes we walked miles along the top track to Heber's Ghyll to listen to the rushing waterfalls and then follow the zig-zag path down over endless bridges, finding stepping stones. After man-made Manningham streets and upright walls the moors, the distance and the trees our world changed overnight.

Holidays might have been few and far between but were so precious. Our very restricted lives hemmed us in, but now the world opened out into a wonderland of new sights and sounds, smells, people and adventure. Discipline was relaxed if not our clothing, and training forgotten and we had a feeling of being on equal terms in the family. Father too, cast aside his Edwardian copy-book self and we were allowed to be ourselves at last. Those happy joyful days can never be forgotten.

CHAPTER VII
EMIGRATION

We had all the usual ailments of the time, mumps following on from whooping-cough, colds, coughs and stomach upsets. In the early days of the century the doctor came to the house but first you had to call with a message at his home where he had a surgery and dispensed his own medicines. The word HOSPITAL was as fearful as the WORKHOUSE. Our doctor made his rounds with a horse and trap taking with him his small daughter who held the reins in his absence. He was only called upon as a last resort for there were bills to pay which was an added worry when money was tight. Mothers used simple handed-down home remedies and did their best.

But this had its advantages for you were nursed at home in your own bed with a fire in the room and everything familiar and your mother at hand to comfort you. You not only had special care and your own toys to play with but all the fussing made you feel a Very Important Person. You were cossetted with beef tea, bread and milk, rice puddings, a raw egg beaten up with milk and sugar and of course your bottle of medicine at the bedside with the doses marked off up the side.

The illness itself might be unpleasant but it was never frightening as it must have been for children who had to have an appendix or tonsils out on the kitchen table. This was common practice with little preparation other than a bare room and a deal of scrubbing. The doctor was your good friend who sat on the bed and chatted. He knew all about you and your family and had probably brought you into the world. Home confinements were the regular thing with relatives or the midwife called in to help. In our walk of life a "monthly nurse" came to live in and stayed to see the new baby well established. She came on a fixed date and often had to fill in several days before the baby arrived - getting underfoot as she was not employed to do housework. Most Friends' babies were delivered by Nurse Oddy, herself a Quaker, dressed in neat uniform, cape and bonnet. When our first little boy cousin was born we saw a lot of her and it was almost like having a Nannie of our own which we read about in the story books; only it didn't last long enough.

With Uncle being a chemist we were given medicines from his

shop. Mother was prone to headaches and we watched her tip into her mouth two special powders folded meticulously in blue and white packets before a drink of water. Uncle rolled his own pills at the back of the shop on a special fluted tray, and provided us with his own version of cod-liver-oil, the great stand-by and cure-all. His white mixture was so drowned with almond essence it was almost worse than the genuine yellow oil and would not go down. He also supplied us with bent glass tubes so we could suck up our iron tonic without staining our teeth. Seidlitz powders, Veno's cough cure, Bella Donna plasters, mustard leaf and linseed poultices were his province rather than the doctor's.

Bread poultices were used for any inflammation. Bread mashed up in scalding water was spread over a piece of linen and quickly slammed on the site then covered with flannel and a bandage to keep in the heat - and repeated at intervals. I still shudder at the memory of a "gathered" thumb which took weeks to cure ending in my wearing a finger-poke that tied round the wrist until the old nail came off and a new one had grown. For coughs camphorated oil was rubbed well into the chest, or if you could get it, goosegrease on brown paper was fastened round you at night. I suffered a green-stick fracture after a fall and was considerably proud of my splinted finger. Whooping-cough was a deadly affliction lasting weeks and wearing out both parents. Mother must have had a tiring time of it looking after the two of us, burning creosote during the night. She kept a special wide white enamel bowl for us to be sick into which we called "the spitting trough". Later on it was kept for work in the garden, as a souvenir.

Living as we did near Lister's mill an area crowded with small houses all with smoking chimneys from coal fires, Father in his enlightenment felt we should benefit by some country air and move higher out of town. He was a man before his time, particularly interested in health and science and was given to experimenting with food and drink. A certain Dr. Ragbagliati (known as Dr. Rab.) himself a member of the Society of Friends, had a practice in Manningham and Father followed his thinking to the letter. A wiry, wizened little man who sat in the Minister's gallery, his head resting on the knob of his stick, who spoke all too long and frequently, he was well-known to us. I think he was the advance guard of the Nature Cure Movement believing in few but herbal remedies. He swore by only two meals a day, no tea or coffee and only homeopathic pills. His enormous volume "Air, food and exercise" was Father's Bible; *we* used it for pressing flowers!

Father used his methods without question and sometimes brought the kitchen scales to table to weigh his meals. He must have been a difficult man to feed with his 'l'eau-d'eau' (a name of his own invention) which was hot water with a little milk and quite tasteless. No alcoholic drink of any sort came into the house or passed his lips, but the tale goes that once at a party somewhere he asked for a second helping of trifle saying "This is very good indeed", quite unaware it was soused with sherry.

Being so keen on good healthy living it was not surprising that he looked for a better place to live. And in March 1908 we moved out to the back of beyond to Toller Drive, just beyond the Hare and Hounds Inn in Heaton.

Now this was a courageous, even outrageous thing to do. Three miles from Forster Square, in the wilds, at the very edge of habitation, among fields, woods and quarries he deposited his family for better or worse. People said "The man's mad!" There were no shops nearer than Duckworth Lane where the trams began, a good twelve minutes walk away, a few similar houses scattered along Toller Lane but where Haworth Road began just nothing in sight but real country, field upon field criss-crossed with stone walls as far as the eye could see.

He rented No. 11, hearing about it from a fellow-Friend living opposite who was best man at his wedding. It was a magnificent idea and showed wisdom and fore-thought. It proved the perfect thing to do. It may have given Mother and Father a deal more work and walking but it was country and over 700 feet high and the air was clear. From the front window you looked out on to Ilkley Moor nine miles away and the strong west winds came direct from Morecambe. We were told if you licked the outside of the windows you could taste the salt from the sea. And there we were on a hill four-storeys high. It was like living in a lighthouse. The houses had gardens, there were fields all round and Heaton Woods less than five minutes walk away and wild, wild winds. And we all flourished.

One thing however came to an end - a triviality. At Athol Road we lived in a network of houses. We knew all the streets round about, the back-to-backs, those with little gardens or flights of steps. It was all rather like a chess board in squares with chapels and shops, churches and the mill as pieces. This was our familiar stamping ground. If Father felt energetic and had nothing better to do he would announce "Come on. Let's go for a Penny Walk". We'd put on our caped coats, our tight beaver hats and gloves and set out.

"Heads to the right, tails to the left", he declared and tossed a penny. Then off we went into the unknown stopping at every corner to make the next move and meandering all over the district as the penny took us.

Now, Penny Walks came to a stop. It was all fields with no footpaths, wide open spaces and sky. Instead we had wind and weather and real country life - and more freedom - and life began afresh.

Winifred and Kathleen (author) with their parents.

CHAPTER VIII
A NEW WORLD

Imagine it, a fairy tale come to life! I couldn't say "Just like a pantomime" for I'd never seen one; theatres played no part in our lives any more than smoking or cards. But it was very like Alice through the Looking Glass" - and that we did know about. This was us climbing through a mirror into a completely different world. Quite unbelievable.

Seventy-four years later I don't have to think hard about it. I'm there in reality living it over again, a shy little girl of eight.

It was a very tall house built on a hillside with four sets of windows in front and only three at the back. The houses were in twos, not in one long row. We had three doors, a front, a back and a side door into the cellar. And it had a garden with trees in it. There were steps everywhere. We ran up and down counting them - 15 to the first landing, 13 more to the attics and then 12 down to the cellar not forgetting 4 more about the place. That made 44. And there was a verandah at the front door, a coloured glass door far bigger than at 52 and the tops of all the windows were the same only with pictures of birds on them. The stairs were open, not walled in, with bannister rails and polished posts top and bottom. This was better than Grandpa's - and we had a separate w.c!

Our twin iron beds were in the back bedroom where we got all the sun. "Directly ahead at mid-day" said Father. There was plenty of room for furniture and the wardrobe was let into the wall. Mother and Father's double bed in the front looked out to miles and miles of country. No houses stood in the way and that was why Father had chosen No. 11. The moors ran right across the windows and behind them lay Ilkley. You could even see the tip of Saltaire Mills chimney hidden by trees, Baildon Moor was like a saucer turned upside down with a road round the edge - that was where Shipley Glen and the railway were and we knew about them.

It was all so exciting we didn't know where to go first. Two large attics had beams reaching to the floor from the roof and you had to be careful not to bump your head. One was to be our playroom, a special room all to ourselves! From the window you could see the quarry down in the fields with its three giant posts meeting at the top where they hoisted up the stone to saw into pieces. We could hear the puffing of the engine all day long. But the cellar was like an underground dungeon with a grid for daylight. This was our wash-kitchen with a black coal range, our mangle and peggy tub and a copper that worked by gas! There were gas-brackets all over the walls of the house. Some had the mantle in a glass bowl underneath not like the upright ones we were used to. New incandescent mantles had to be taken very carefully out of their cardboard tubes and set fire before they gave out a light and we never dare touch them. But we still had our candles and tapers. Mother kept her kitchen tapers in a fish paste jar tied up with a bootlace.

As for the garden - the new garden that first day was something never to be forgotten. Besides we could run in and out from the kitchen without any hats on. First came the flat part lovely for tops and skipping, then little paths and steps up a hill to the top with three small sycamore trees in a row. In between was the 'lawn' which Father had to cut with a lawn-mower. It wasn't long before he started netting hammocks to stretch between the trees, "But not for swinging on, remember, just lying in". Over the stone wall at the end was a haystack and a field and nothing else but sky. The walls were just like the Cow and Calf rocks to touch. It was all a dream and not one scrap like Athol Road. At once we got that special holiday feeling of space and freedom.

Oh, the things there were to discover! Funny electric bells in every room, round wood stumps set in the wall, even one over the bath. You pressed a button in the middle and it set a red flag wagging in the kitchen - this, or course, was if you kept a maid. We didn't but we went all over the house pressing buttons. These weren't like Grandma's pulled by wires, but were electric worked by a battery Uncle George said. We had no one to answer the bell, only Mrs. Bogg who didn't count. She came to clean and sat in the kitchen with her little boy sometimes when Mother and Father went out. How we teased her, till we got the giggles then she'd say "You'll cry before the night's out". And sure enough we did.

Every day brought new adventures. Father sowed packets of Shirley poppies everywhere and when they flowered they looked like 'hundreds and thousands'. We had to buy new things like deck-chairs, garden tools, long clothes-lines to stretch in two directions, and a watering can which was good fun as we each had our own garden. But the great thing was cutting the grass. There was a very steep bank sloping up to the trees, a 'one-in-one' Father called it. Just how to cut the grass? With much puffing and heavy breathing he rushed the mower over the lawn and up as far as he could reach and it slid down of its own accord. Doing this all the way along tired him but then he had to start all over again lowering the machine from the top and dragging it back. Sometimes we used to help by standing at the top hauling on a rope. But what we liked best was sliding down on a tea-tray when the grass was dry.

That first year we had lots of garden parties with the four grandparents in bonnets and mantles and perhaps the folding silk screen and sunshades, while the uncles were busy taking photos. We had four amateur photographers in the family and we loved to be allowed to sit in the dark boxroom with a candle burning in a red-glass lantern, watching for the picture on the glass plate to appear as the hypo tipped in the white tray. I can't remember having picnics on the lawn but we did have our dinners out on the kitchen table. And for special visitors out came the old bamboo tea-table with the four sliding panels and an embroidered tablecloth. When Father bought us a small-sized croquet set our cup of happiness was full.

But what I didn't like was 'the night-soil-men' who came when we were in bed. Our ash-pit was at the top of the side path; it was a stone cell with a stable door. You threw your rubbish in at the top door and the men cleared it out at the bottom. Our side path was very steep and wide with a big iron gate. The men brought their horse and cart up the path and then shovelled the rubbish in. That was bad enough but they had to back the horse up and this meant a great hullabaloo getting it into position. In the dark this was very frightening. Sister Winifred used to climb out of bed and peep under the blind and revelled in it but I put my head under the clothes. It was truly a nightmare. Later Father bought a load of logwood chips from a mill, which had been used for dyeing and this made our path quite silent and smart so we began to call it a 'drive'.

We never tired of our garden with all its space and hillside, but life must go on and Mother had to walk to the nearest shops at Duckworth Lane. Here trams ran from the tramsheds into Forster Square, down Whetley Hill. This was so steep we often thought one might run off the lines. Trams had open staircases at both ends where the driver stood, so he only had to walk through for the journey back. At the terminus the trolley had to be unhooked from one overhead wire and clicked on to the other. To clear the way the driver clanged his foot-bell and if anyone was in danger of getting run-over he let down the cow-catcher with a frightening clatter. We liked to go upstairs, not in the middle covered part but outside where you could lean over and see everything. The backs of the slatted seats could be tipped either way. That journey from country to town cost one penny.

Toller Lane was quite narrow and hardly used. After all it only led to Haworth or else to Bingley so only horse-drawn farm carts and quarry wagons were on the road. We had never heard the word 'traffic'. The Hare and Hounds was a landmark being the last inn out of Bradford. Toller Drive was the first turn left after that. If we used a cab we told the driver to look out for the Hare and Hounds. "Oh, aye," he'd say, "Ah know yon. Dog an' Ratten". The round toll bar stood at the end of Leylands Lane with its watchful windows on all sides. I thought it must be lovely to live in. Otherwise there were no houses of any sort save a few like ours and some back-to-back cottages beyond the inn. You could stand at the corner where Haworth and Bingley Roads met and there was nothing but bare fields and quarries. We were on the boundary though Heaton was a little village on its own with Heaton Hill a view-point. You could walk miles and never meet a soul but we did have a blacksmith's nearby and we used to spend a lot of time standing in the doorway watching the large blacksmith at work and were never turned away. The shoeing of the horses, the sparks, the sigh of the bellows and music of the anvil are as much a part of my life as if I was a Dales child.

I think our far-off houses were treated a 'bit special' because the greengrocer and the butcher called early morning for orders and they were delivered by bicycle before dinner. The milkman had his own farm in Cottingley, a long way to come. His milk float was drawn by a white mare who knew exactly where to turn or stop. Mr. Hill carried several churns and tipped the milk into his metal pail with a pint and a gill measure slung over the side. He ladled it into your basin and this was put on one side for the cream to rise. Mother always had cream in her tea, so she took a large spoon and skimmed it off the surface. Mr. Hill came all weathers and in deep snow looked so tired she sometimes dosed him with sal volatile, having no brandy of course in the house.

Father being a great walker soon had us out in the woods and fields. We walked miles in our hats, coats and boots with Mother in her long full skirt that touched the ground so the hem was lined with brush-braid. Father took to a straw benjie out of office hours. We went in all directions, Goit Stock, Miles Rough, St. Ives, Cottingley, Chellow Dene where the sight of those terrible boat-hooks taught us to keep away from the edge. But our favourite haunt was Heaton Woods. They were quite wild then and Father thought nothing of damming up the stream with clods of earth and stones while we jumped about and Mother as usual sat and watched. We climbed the steep sides, looked for the red beck and made our way up to Six Days Only dodging the water that gushed down both sides of the winding lane that followed the high flagged pathway. Further along was Dungeon Woods with more slippery slopes to test our feet. You would never believe we were little town children brought up on pavements.

Winters were exciting too as we both had sledges and found plenty of hills to slide down. The best place was Heights Lane, very steep and very empty. Mother, of course, accompanied us and watched while we shot from top to bottom. I fancy we had it all to ourselves. Snow drifted wall-high along Toller Lane as we went to the shops, rain sliced down with no shelter and the Pennine winds blew us off course. But we were well protected in our black rubber mackintoshes and sou-westers and had snow-boots fastening on over our shoes, and gaiters that buttoned all the way up. Button-hooks were a part of our daily lives.

We also had summers and sunsets, rainbows and shadows across Baildon Moor and lovely green tents of leaves in the woods. All so different from the forbidding straight lines of Manningham streets. With a garden and flowers to pick, hollow trees to explore, birds and bird-song and all that fresh air and outdoor life we soon turned from little town dwellers into country children, happy and rosy-cheeked. All due to Father's wise thinking.

CHAPTER IX
FUN & GAMES

We hadn't many toys when we were children, there weren't many about. Dolls of course, of different sizes all beautifully dressed by Mother and Auntie Marie; the baby's long clothes were a copy of the real thing, barracoat, binder, bonnet with a swansdown brim, the lot. They were very real companions with china faces you could wash, fine hair to comb and smooth jointed limbs. But oh how jealous I was of Winifred's big doll Dorothy, so much bigger and better than my Mildred. We had prams too with the sample blankets from the warehouse and covers made of flannel all jimped and embroidered. Her pram too was bigger than mine, with a reversible hood. Another source of envy.

Father made us a dolls house with all the right furniture and Mother saw to our little stuffed dolls with all-china heads including the black hair. Come to think of it our main play was 'houses' or 'mothers and fathers'. A dust sheet draped over the biggest clothes-horse was big enough to get inside and imagination did the rest. On special occasions we were allowed to play with Father's dolls which were normally shut away in his big Gladstone bag, so we had plenty of scope for acting out stories. In about 1905 teddy bears came into being, named after Teddy Roosevelt the American President. Now they were something completely different and how I longed for one as we never had a pet in the house. I remember one day at Grandma's I was given one as a surprise. It completely overwhelmed me and I was so happy I burst into tears. They all said with complete lack of understanding "What are you crying for? Don't you like it?" I have it still and it's just as loveable.

There were balls, or course, all alike and plain rubber, but a ball makes a good playmate anywhere. Battledores and shuttlecocks came out at Easter, also whips and tops to be spun on the pavements. Our battledores were banjo-shaped, covered with parchment like a drum and were musical when tapped. Skipping ropes were always in season. I was given a very superior one with ball-bearings in the handles so the rope never twisted; I had to guard this diligently. Girls' hoops were made of wood; boys' were of heavy iron with the iron handle fastened on so they made a horrible clatter. I thought little of them, they were a poor do - but then I specialised in hoop tricks. Mine was so large I could set it going, bend double and run through it on the move time after time.

Some outdoor games were played in groups - hopscotch, statues, pise-ball, 'up for Monday' and hide-and-seek. 'IT' was chosen by one person thumping a circle of outstretched fists saying "One potato, two potatoes, three potatoes, four . . ." and ending "1, 2, 3, and out goes she". One thing at Athol Road that never palled was bursting tar bubbles in the road in the hot sun. This was too tempting to resist though we knew we would get into trouble at home when Mother had to clean up our shoes and fingers. At Toller Drive we got round to celebrating Plot Night, a very private affair. We all sat, grandparents included, at our bedroom window wrapped in rugs, while Father put on a harmless show on the lawn, spectacular it might have been but there weren't many bangs. Another event that will never fade was when we had a deep snowfall and Father built us a real snow igloo we could get into. *And* he burnt a real candle in it at night which lit up the inside. He really did know how to amuse children - and enjoyed himself into the bargain. Being taken into the garden once in the pitch-dark to see Haley's comet at our bedtime was something never to be forgotten.

We were well supplied with indoor games as Father was very partial to them. Board games like Halma, Parchesi, Ludo and Draughts, also puzzles, dominoes, spillikins and tiddly-winks. No playing cards were allowed in the house but there was always Snap (and smiling snap), happy families, beggar-my neighbour bringing with it the smart of being left 'old maid' and you knew you would never marry. One of our very special things was a very practical affair, an ideal present for children of any age - a set of Uncle's wooden chemist's drawers from the shop. They were made in mahogany and well polished and were in rows, some twenty of them. They had names printed in gold on the front arranged in alphabetical order - Alum, Bac Junip, Camomile, Soda Bic, all very enticing but we had no idea what they meant. We kept our doll's clothes in them and one would say "Where is Mildred's red cape?" to be told "Look in Mag Sulph". They lasted years and couldn't have been improved upon.

At children's parties (which were few and far between) we wore white frilly full dresses with broad sashes tied in a bow at the back with fringe on the ends. Some lucky little girls wore dancing slippers with elastic criss-crossing down their stockings. Not so the Binns girls who had plain serviceable brown shoes and, of course, long woollen stockings. We played games like 'Turn the trencher' - (the round bread board) which you spun round calling out someone's name who had to rescue it before it fell. There was Postman's Knock, The Parson's cat, Hide the thimble, Musical Chairs, and a riotous affair called Family Coach where each person was given a part of a coach and four and had to get up and turn round when your name was mentioned in a story. It was at parties you showed off with your special 'party-piece' either a recitation or a piano solo, but I was too shy and hid myself away.

Books? Not many but read over and over again. About the Nesbit family, "A peep behind the scenes", and Mrs. Molesworth stories not forgetting the new Beatrix Potter books which were so different and everybody's favourite. There were also thin paper-backed stories very moral and sad like "Little Meg's Children" or "Eric, or Little by Little", and often they frightened you with kidnappings. Mother took a weekly paper called Home Chat which had a jolly children's page called Jungle Jinks that went on for years. But reading was never encouraged at home. It was a question of "Get something to do, do!" and occupations were provided. Small wonder as Mother had been an assistant at a needlework counter she soon got us busy with needle and thread so we were well in advance of other children with our hemming and feather-stitching, knitting and crochet. I've always been grateful for this early training in using my hands and my whole life has centred round craft work.

The grown-ups had their musical evenings when we were in bed. Our family could muster two pianists and two flautists and we all sang readily. Friends from the Meeting supplied a cello and violin and Father collected and filed all the classical music sheets. Social evenings were arranged at the Meeting House including music and an Essay and Discussion Society. These were held in the large Institute room upstairs where there was a queer sofa that took my fancy. It seated four, was upholstered and faced four different ways which I thought rather odd. There were singsongs round the piano whenever the family met together with Grandpa Spinks harmonising in the bass. He had a fine voice and was conductor at the Adult School with his own ivory conducting stick. My sister was no mean accompanist at an early age and enjoyed showing off with Father or Uncle George with their flutes. We both took piano lessons as a matter of course, but I never 'shaped' and practising was a penance.

Christmas was looked forward to all the year. As our house was now the largest it was Mother who bore the brunt of holding our famous family parties. The work and organisation rested entirely on her shoulders. She saved up for it all the year having rows of little

42

boxes labelled, Christmas, Window Cleaner, Holidays, Presents, set aside from housekeeping money. There were as many as fifteen of us, and three generations either staying in the house or coming for days. It was enormous fun with the cousins to play with and everyone in holiday mood. Even Great-Aunt Eliza from the Almshouses rose to heights of merriment though normally very sour.

The work involved must have been a nightmare with everything home-made but Mother never complained, just saying at the end of one day "My brain won't work any more." All work was multiplied by four and she had to be very inventive; when filling the stone hot-water bottles at night she not only lit the cellar copper but warmed them in the oven first to retain the heat - until one night when a stopper was left in and there was a terrific explosion which nearly wrecked that indispensable oven.

The meals were the biggest headache requiring weeks of work beforehand making the puddings and cakes, the bread, pies and all the special Christmas dainties. I clearly remember the Ceremony of the Sponge-cakes. The big yellow baking bowl 18 inches across was first warmed in the oven together with the sugar, and all the cake tins lined with paper. Then Mother actually did 'take twenty eggs' (as Mrs. Beaton had it) and we literally did beat them with the sugar for half an hour *by hand*. Yes, by hand, the naked hand! We children were anxious to help, we set the alarm clock and took it in turns but it was well worth it for the scraping out of the bowl afterwards. All our food was kept in the larder down twelve steps and how many times Mother went up and down in the course of a day has never been recorded. The pace quickened as Christmas drew near and all the shelves were neatly stored with every possible thing from turkey and sausages to mince-pies and jellies, for there were many mouths to feed. It must have been a gruelling time, though when the day came she had plenty of helpers in 'siding up' and 'washing the pots'. There were times in the morning when she sent all the men and children out for a walk to get them from underfoot. Imagine entertaining the entire family the hard Edwardian way! But we five children only thought of it as endless fun and the peak of the year.

We never had a Christmas tree, just a wassail-bob made from three wooden butter-tub hoops tricked out with crinkle paper and decorations kept on the wardrobe top the rest of the year. Holly and mistletoe were laid over each picture and roaring fires lit in every room. Our stockings were only a gesture and we knew exactly what to expect - an apple, an orange (a great seasonal treat), a cracker, some sweets and chocolate money wrapped in gold paper with a new penny in the toe. Father got the proverbial lump of coal. We couldn't seat everyone at the big dining table even with the two leaves in, so some of us children sat alone, very importantly at a corner table.

Our present-giving came in the afternoon when all the traces of the big turkey dinner had been cleared away. This again was a Family Institution and what J.B. Priestley would call High Jinks, for the two funny uncles always provided some ridiculous happening. Each year 'the presentation' you might call it, was something different and utterly silly. We all went into the sitting-room with our parcels wrapped in good brown paper and string from the warehouse and piled them on a rug in the middle of the floor. Then sat round a blazing fire waiting excitedly for the Event. It was kept a close secret and each year was better than the last. Once it was a school prize-giving and the uncles in cap and gown, with thought-up props, handed out parcels to the winners. "To Grannie Spinks for winning the high jump" and "This for baby Ralph for the loudest cry of the year". On one memorable occasion they thought up a sausage machine that distributed presents. Our large knife-cleaning machine from the kitchen was put on a table covered with a long cloth. One uncle dressed as a magician turned the handle and a parcel shot out from under the table. Oh how we children loved it all.

That was only the beginning. After that we began to open our presents starting with the youngest while we all watched and waited our turn. We never missed a trick. It took the whole afternoon but it never palled. Father, always provident and very practical brought in a clothes basket into which went all the paper and string. On Boxing Day it was his self-imposed task to straighten them all out and tie the string into little knots for future use. Nothing was ever wasted.

That was only one of our junketings. In the evening after a sit-down tea we always played tip-it, consequences and drawing games which were quite hilarious as our musical cushion or percussion bands using cooking utensils. It was laughter and fun all along the way and invariably ended up with charades. No ordinary charades ours. These were run by the two uncles who chose their teams and did all the plotting. We dressed up in anything we could lay our hands on, always finding a fez, a ballet tu-tu, red noses and false moustaches and the key-words were invariably forgotten. Mother always laughed till she cried but Father was rather left out. He didn't possess the Spinks family sense of humour and clowning, besides he was stock-taking at the warehouse and working long hours and was tired. He took to his bed early with 'pobs' and was hardly missed in the racket and laughter.

On Boxing Day it all started again and we had a second day of buffoonery and fun. More of Mother's marvellous meals, then at tea we always came down in impromptu fancy-dress which started the ball rolling even earlier. More games and singing and charades and we had a second night of revelry. I've often thought since that for a Quaker family we could outclass any other in noise, song, wit and daftness — yet never any smoking or drinking and nothing stronger than home-made lemonade. Strange, that though theatres were verboten we put on fancy costumes and acted for hours on end!

Oh our family Christmases, how we enjoyed them - and showed it. Manners and morals were forgotten and everyone was in a mad happy mood. What an anti-climax afterwards to be just Father and Mother and two little girls in a quiet and ordered atmosphere. It all came true, "Christmas comes but once a year . . ."

CHAPTER X
THE THREE R's

Having a sister three years older works both ways. She can lead the way and teach you all the tricks, but she's also streets ahead and you can never catch up. So maybe I was a little spoilt but still trailed behind and felt sorry for myself. Two small things gave me a boost - Mother said I folded my nightgown better than she did, and I said "white" correctly while she called it "wite".

So school was no surprise as I was prepared in advance by all her tales. We first went to a little private school off Oak Lane run by a German lady, Miss Bruning. Bradford had quite a large German community in Edwardian days. She spoke with a decided accent and we started off the morning with the Lord's Prayer in German . . . "Vater unser der du bist in Himmel . . ." She also kept lodgers and there was a peculiar smell about the place I didn't like. I later discovered this was sauerkraut. This was strongest in the kitchen and we had to go through there to reach the 'double-you' outside. One little girl we knew vowed she never once used it during her schooldays there - but then she lived virtually next door.

It was very much a Kindergarten though we sat at long backless desks arranged round the sides of the fireplace. We mostly learnt from wall picture maps with the teacher picking out her talk with a pointer. I still remember one about the life-story of the apple all in colour. The piano was in her sitting-room where we stood motionless in a semi-circle on the white drugget laid down to protect her carpet. We learnt to read the alphabet way C-A-T spells CAT but I've no recollection of any number work. For writing there were round inkwells sunk into the desk tops but beginners started on slates in wooden frames. The thin grey pencils were also slate and screeched like a murder of birds when you pressed on. But at least you could rub out your mistakes with a wet sponge.

I realise now what a large part the five senses play in any child's life. Those slates were not only cold and noisy but the sponges too had a nasty smell, no doubt due to old age and hot hands. We were promoted slowly from capitals to pothooks but rarely got round to words. In the afternoon we had 'kindergarten' which was an extra, so with non-paying parents this meant reading. We carefully threaded strips of coloured paper into slotted paper squares and thought it wonderful. Or we made pen-wipers out of red flannel in the shape of a poppy to give to our fathers. There was clay too in an outhouse, needing a second apron; that was very messy and again had a horrid smell. My chief memory of the young assistant was her hands. She stood behind leaning over us when correcting our work and I couldn't take my eyes from those long tapering fingers with pointed nails. Everyone in our family had thick ugly hands and I always had an eye for the beautiful. Miss Bruning's was a smart double-fronted house set back from the road and very superior; all the ones we went into were in rows or back-to-backs.

The move to Heaton meant a different school. This time we went together as new girls in our tam-o-shanters and buttoned boots with a tucket-purse slung round our necks. This was another private school but less old-fashioned. It took about five minutes to get there and at first Mother accompanied us as Toller Lane was so lonely. There were just a few houses like ours then fields both sides, very exposed in bad weather. We always made a point of jumping on the milestone half way to Duckworth Lane, to look for Lister's mill and that special chimney. On the other side was a huge advertisement hoarding stretching the length of the cricket field at the back. In two-foot-high painted capitals it spelt out EMPIRE TONIGHT 6-50 and 9 GRAND STAR PERFORMANCES ALL THE YEAR ROUND. This always had to be spelt out and shortened the walk.

All the children round about came here and we began to make friends outside the Quaker circle and found out how other people lived their lives. We had separate desks here and now began to write in pen and ink with scratchy nibs. First, between double lines in exercise books making rows of pothooks with thin upstrokes and thick downstrokes. Then came copying out one line of words all down the page. Great store was set on perfect hand-writing and we were marked on results, aiming for "Excellent ★ ★". We chanted out tables in chorus and recited in most lessons, things like "York, capital Yorkshire on the Ouse. London, capital England on the Thames".

Again memories are emotional rather than educational. The children stayed till twelve but I was with the 8-year-olds which included some naughty boys. Now we were an all-girl family and I knew nothing about the ways of boys. It was a real eye-opener. At home we had learnt to keep well in the background and toe the line and the daring behaviour of those boys flabberghasted me; though they were probably normal enough. Punishment for misbehaviour was to have your knuckles rapped. The boys held out their hands face down and the teacher brought her thick ridged marking pencil down smartly where it hurt most. It hurt me too in sympathy and I decided never to do anything wrong at school. At least one was safe at home.

This safety business was our undoing. We were brought up on reins always secure and cared for, obeying Father's many directions. So we stifled our feelings. No tantrums, no tears but never free to experiment or fight our own battles. When we exchanged visits with the rest of the family in Athol Road we were accompanied by a grown-up though it was fully half an hour's walk each way. So it was roundabouts and swings. We loved living in Heaton on the edge of habitation but found it a lonely business.

Our education didn't end after school, there were things to learn about on all sides. We found Toller Drive had once been a track to a day-pit for surface coal and was S-shaped to allow the horses to pull carts up the steep rise. The houses were built on quarry land and we picked up lots of broken clay-pipe stems, but never any bowls in the soil. We learnt the names of the trees in Heaton Woods and Mother was keen on stars and took us out in the dark to point out the constellations and follow the quarters of the moon. Father, who strode the moors told us he could walk from our front door to the Grove in Ilkley via Dick Hudson's in just three hours so he took us all over the district. We often went through the woods to Saltaire to explore the what was to us, giantsized toy village with its 'Salt School' and mill, almshouse and shops, church and bridge and even its own station. It was well worth the long toil on foot and we came back by train. So too was Shipley Glen with its open toast-rack railway that both frightened and delighted us as it swung dangerously over the spinning bobbins on a wire rope. From so many places we could see Lister's chimney in the distance or the clump of trees at the top of Haworth Road. We learnt our geography the easy way.

Even about Bradford. Auntie Marie now lived in Great Horton near Uncle's new shop and we often went to see her. Instead of taking a tram into town and out on the opposite side, Mother took a short cut from Toller Lane down to Thornton Road and then up Ingleby Road. This was extremely boring, all houses and mills but we were marched along willy-nilly. So she invented a game to keep us going. We hunted for and counted (in competition) every hair-pin we saw on the pavement, for ladies wore their long hair combed back over chignons and their hair-pins were always dropping out. Trust Mother to find a way out.

Going by tram to Leeds was another piece of education. Forster

Square was the starting point for most trams so passengers queued up between railings we called 'sheep-pens' in the very centre. We all wandered freely about which shows how empty and safe the roads were. Now the Leeds tramline gauge was different from Bradford's so at the halfway mark at Stanningley the tram slowed down and laboriously, inch by inch, the driver levered aside the wheels to alter the span - and on we went without changing.

When we went into town we made for the markets. The Saturday Market was a real country one selling puppies, and cage-birds, hens and rabbits. But Kirkgate was always open and packed with interest. Everything you could wish for without spending a ha-penny - toys, books, music, hats, corsets, shoes, flowers, you could fill in half an hour just wandering up and down the aisles. But oh! how we longed to eat at one of the pie-and-peas stalls with their narrow tables and seats like pews. But we had to be satisfied with standing over the iron grids in the floor letting the hot air run up our legs.

We had got used to our new life in Heaton when Winifred went off to boarding school. That altered everything. She soon settled in and enjoyed herself but it brought my life to a full stop. No more companionship, no more stories in bed, no one of my own age at home and only me in the big bath. I felt alone for the first time in my life and it was dreadful. That first night Mother and Father put up my single bed in their room so I didn't keep awake crying. But even that was strange and unsettling. Never before had I seen Father dressing in the morning or Mother in her curling pins. I kept my eyes on the painted birds in the centre of the stained-glass window tops - and to this day the sight of them brings on that terrible lost feeling.

I needn't have worried. I got extra attention and was soon back in our joint room rather enjoying the importance. But now I became Mother's shadow and went round the house sharing her various activities, learning new skills and growing up. I was only nine but I now had to stand on my own feet and invent games for myself. The toy mangle had been discarded but Mother bought me a toy cooking stove with an oven and two pans on top. With her usual sound common sense she didn't let me use flour but crushed biscuit crumbs so all the concoctions I thought up could really have been eaten. It was satisfying too to have things my way instead of falling in with Big Sister's ideas. And Mother had more time to teach me about housework. I helped stitch the newly-washed valances on to the bed-sides, slipped the collar supports into the high necks of her blouses, put on clean starched pillowcases pushing the bone studs into their button-holes, scoured the front steps with whitestone from the ironmongers leaving a neat chalk-like edge and helped clean up after the mucky sweep - and loved it all.

In fact I was in my element making and doing - knitting Grandpa's yard-long garters in white cotton only an inch wide, threading melon seeds, doing embroidery and knitted lace edging, stencilling, painting, making doll's clothes, using Father's round black ruler and his sealing-wax - but the annoying part was waiting always for the secotine or fish-glue to set. All this became a lifelong interest and ended up with me designing craft work for women's magazines and occupational therapy in hospital. This all due to Mother's patience and skills. So this period became a flowering of my creative abilities instead of the barren loneliness it first appeared.

Besides, school holidays were an exciting reunion when Winifred came home full of impossible school tales Angela Brazil would have envied. About how they had to drink cold milk from big jars for breakfast and tea, grab a hunk of dry bread in passing on the way down to the recess bathe. Only half an hour allowed to undress, swim across at least once, dry and dress and run round the Great Garden hair wet and flapping. Or skipping in long lines "All in together, 1-2-3"; roller skating on the playground, even Saturday pennies to spend. I learnt all the school slang, heard about the teachers' nicknames and her friends, and their goings-on. And squirmed when she told me how the girls would collect in the stone corridors chanting "Let's mob Flea! Let's mob Flea!" - Flea being a much-hated Mistress on Duty who chivvied them about out of lesson hours. I knew it all and could even recite the Saturday night list of clothing sent to wash - "Handkerchieves, stockings, chemises, linings or knickers, stays or stay-bodices, combinations". So much so that more than once I was threatened with "You can't go to Ackworth if you're going to be a cry-baby", reversing the bogeyman story. For the bogeyman of the time was the 'Board Man' who came to take little children away to school - or rather he came to the house to make enquiries about absence.

When you're young you're learning something fresh every day and it's all adventure. This was to be another adventure, though not a frightening one for most of our family had been to this Quaker School near Pontefract. Father, Uncle George, Cousin Alfred, Grandpa and even Great-grandmother, so it was a familiar place. We went over to see Winifred perhaps once a term with a long train journey, and a longer walk at both ends of a long day. I knew too it would be a tough life with no mollycoddling, but it was the right and proper thing to do.

50

But when the day came there was a sick feeling in my tummy. Leaving home for the first time for twelve long weeks. Leaving all the people and things I loved. And only Winifred to turn to and she was now high in the school and above bothering with a second-form girl.

The cab came to the door, our two trunks were strapped on but I didn't get that holiday feeling. I was a very sad, shy little girl who said goodbye at the station, joining the group of other scholars from Bradford. There had been goodbyes round all the family with a special hug for my special Grandpa and a last kissemy-smacker at home. And now I was to be just No. 40 in a crowd of three hundred.

This was to be my second home for six happy years. And although it made me cry I knew in my heart of hearts it was not going to be so much a change of life but a larger family I was joining at this Quaker school. I belonged there.

*Uncle George (the chemist), his wife Marie
(Mother's sister), parents, Winifred and Kathleen.*